BETTING FOR PROFIT

BETTING FOR PROFIT

*Flat Racing and National Hunt
Systems to help you win*

by
**"STATISTICIAN"
DAVID DUNCAN**

W. FOULSHAM & CO. LTD
LONDON · NEW YORK · TORONTO · CAPE TOWN · SYDNEY

W. FOULSHAM & COMPANY LIMITED
Yeovil Road, SLOUGH, Berkshire SL1 4JH

ISBN 0-572-01123-7
© W. Foulsham & Co. Ltd 1980

Made and printed in Great Britain by
C. Nicholls & Company Ltd.
The Philips Park Press, Manchester

CONTENTS

Introduction

There never was, and I am quite certain there never will be, an infallible racing system. If one could be devised, bookmakers and the Totalisator would cease to exist and the betting element in the sport would certainly be dead. On the other hand, there is a world of difference between planned, systematic betting and haphazard punting according to fancy. The backer who plans his operations methodically stands a chance of winning over a reasonable period. That is my conviction and the object of this book is to suggest ways in which this may be done.

Each chapter is based on a profound study of statistics, backed up by an intimate knowledge of the racing game acquired over many, many years. The whole spectrum of racing is analysed in depth – Flat and National Hunt racing, favourites and outsiders, Classic horses, two-year-olds and handicappers, chasers and hurdlers, the racing press, all come under the microscope. The whole complex question of staking is discussed in detail. In short, this is a book for anyone interested in racing and betting.

There is no guarantee that, having read it, you will suddenly make fantastic profits from your betting. In fact that is unlikely, for the 'glorious uncertainty' of racing will always be present, but for anyone who is prepared to take his sport seriously, the methods outlined in the following pages will certainly be of interest. I hope that they also prove profitable.

SYSTEMS FOR THE FLAT

SYSTEM ONE

The ultimate answer
to the problem of favourites

Systems based on favourites are probably the most popular form of methodical betting on horses. Yet I think it is fair to say that the majority of punters who back nothing but favourites are seldom much richer at the end of the season. The reason, I believe, is that they are unable to discriminate between what are good bets on favourites and what are bad. The ideas outlined below aim to isolate the cream of this type of selection.

As a first step in the absolutely vital process of refinement, I show below the percentage success rate for various kinds of favourites over a recent five-year period:

Nurseries	29% winners
3-y-o handicaps	29% winners
All-age handicaps	28% winners
ALL HANDICAPS	29% Winners
2-y-o non-handicaps	43% winners
3-y-o non-handicaps	40% winners
Weight-for-age	46% winners
ALL NON-HANDICAPS	44% winners
ALL RACES	36% winners

There are obvious conclusions to be drawn from this table. It is evident that handicaps should be left severely alone. On the other hand, non-handicaps of all kinds return a healthy percentage of winners. Hence the first fundamental rule: bet only in non-handicaps.

It is possible to take the study of the statistics of favourites a stage further. Some courses are undeniably better for favourites than others. There follows a table which shows the percentage of winning non-handicap favourites at individual courses over the same five-year period:

1.	FOLKESTONE	56%	19.	NOTTINGHAM	45%
2.	EDINBURGH	54%	20.	BATH	45%
3.	HAYDOCK	53%	21.	CATTERICK	45%
4.	CHEPSTOW	53%	22.	CHESTER	45%
5.	BRIGHTON	51%	23.	YARMOUTH	45%
6.	NEWCASTLE	51%	24.	EPSOM	44%
7.	THIRSK	50%	25.	LEICESTER	44%
8.	PONTEFRACT	49%	26.	DONCASTER	43%
9.	WINDSOR	48%	27.	REDCAR	43%
10.	BEVERLEY	48%	28.	GOODWOOD	43%
11.	WOLVERHAMPTON	47%	29.	NEWMARKET	43%
12.	HAMILTON	47%	30.	WARWICK	43%
13.	STOCKTON	46%	31.	SANDOWN	43%
14.	SALISBURY	46%	32.	YORK	42%
15.	LINGFIELD	45%	33.	ASCOT	42%
16.	CARLISLE	45%	34.	NEWBURY	41%
17.	AYR	45%	35.	KEMPTON	41%
18.	RIPON	45%			

It is obvious that for the most part the top courses, which feature competitive racing between horses of the highest class, have the worst record for favourites. You should, therefore, make it a rule not to bet at the following venues: Ascot, Doncaster, Goodwood, Kempton, Newbury, Newmarket, Redcar, Sandown, Warwick and York.

You will certainly miss winners by adopting this course, but in the long run you will avoid many, many more losers.

So much for statistics for now. The final step in sorting out the best favourites to back is more complex. If I were asked to give one reason why most people who habitually back favourites lose over a reasonable period, I would say that it is because they do not discriminate on grounds of form between one favourite and another. Simply because a horse is made favourite it does not automatically mean that it is a sound wager. Selective form criteria should be applied to a prospective favourite bet just as much as to any other potential racing investment. Obviously this is a matter for individual judgement which can only be learned through experience, but if you adopt the following general principles you will not go far wrong:

Fitness
The only person who can estimate exactly the state of fitness of a horse is its trainer. However, the form student can usually make an educated guess. Whatever a horse has been doing on the training grounds, there is no real substitute for the racecourse test. Any horse which has had a long lay-off since its last public appearance should always be treated with suspicion. Certainly a horse which is having its first run of the season should be avoided. There is no reason why you

13

should gamble on a horse's fitness. There are plenty of other opportunities with horses of proven fitness, which is measured by their recent racecourse performances.

Form

What is meant by 'form' is one of racing's great imponderables. Broadly speaking, you should look for a horse which has produced good recent performances in similar company. As a rule-of-thumb guide, it is a good idea to concentrate only on those horses which were placed first, second, third or fourth last time out. A favourite that could not manage a place on its previous outing is a highly suspect proposition and nine times out of ten the risk is simply not worth taking.

Strength of the Opposition

This is often difficult to estimate. Usually the danger signal is a field packed with winners and seconds last time out. These are the kind of races which often see the favourite upset. As an example, take two hypothetical races:

RACE ONE	RACE TWO
021 A(Favourite)	002 A (Favourite)
221 B	040 B
001 C	041 C
212 D	000 D
100 E	403 E
223 F	300 F
412 G	200 G
114 H	040 H

In my view the favourite in Race Two is a far better proposition than its counterpart in Race One, where almost every horse has the potential form to beat the favourite. A simple count based on performance figures is a rather crude method of estimating the strength of possible dangers. More intensive study of the form of the favourite's rivals, however, will usually confirm first impressions based on this rough test.

Distance

Every horse has invariably a best racing distance, yet for one reason or another does not always compete over that distance. This applies to favourites as much as to any other candidate. A good guide to a horse's distance preferences is the 'D' in brackets after its name which all racing pages use to show that a horse has won over the distance. Except in the case of early-season two-year-olds and maiden races, I would forget any favourite that has not won at least once over the distance of the race under review.

Going

Some horses can perform creditably on all kinds of going. They are, however, exceptions; most horses have a distinct preference. There are some which hate firm ground, some which love it. Others 'come on' 10 lb or more when the ground is on the soft side. The answer to the problem is to be found in the form book, although one sporting daily lists the number of wins a horse has recorded to date and indicates the state of the going on each winning run. This is a quick and largely accurate guide to the type of ground on which a horse produces its best form.

These five form factors are to some extent generalizations. It is up to the backer to examine carefully each point when assessing a favourite's chance and to draw his own conclusions. Sometimes results will confound him, but such a procedure is a useful discipline which more often than not will pay dividends.

Finally it is necessary to say something about prices. No hard-and-fast rule can be formulated, but you should never attempt to 'buy money' on a series of odds on hotpots. In fact, given the current punitive rate of taxation on betting, it is best to avoid any horse likely to start at odds-on. In assessing potential investments always seek to obtain value for money in relation to how you estimate chances. This is not easy at first, but comes with a little experience.

I have said a great deal in a small space, but the burden of my message is clear: favourites can definitely be made to pay. Haphazard punting on this or that market-leader will sometimes win, but more often lose, and discrimination can reap handsome dividends. To summarize my advice:

1: Confine betting to non-handicaps.

2: Certain courses are better for favourites than others. Some are positively bad for favourites.

3: There is nothing magic in the fact that a horse is made favourite. Its chances should be assessed by form criteria just as much as with any other racing investment. Good recent form in similar class is the best guide.

4: In no circumstances bet at odds-on.

As far as staking is concerned, it should be said that favourites are the type of selection which produce a high percentage of winners and relatively short losing runs. This is ideal material with which to use some kind of stake-adjustment formula. (The final section of this book discusses at some length the question of staking.)

SYSTEM TWO

How to pinpoint
the cream of two-year-old bets

Few racing experts would disagree with the view that two-year-old form, particularly in non-handicaps, is more consistently predictable than any other. There are a number of very sound reasons for the reliability in running of the vast majority of good-class juveniles.

First of all, enthusiasm is a typical characteristic of most first-season horses. Once an outing or two has eradicated any tendency to run 'green' through inexperience, a two-year-old that has shown ability can be relied upon to go on reproducing its form from race to race. Mature horses are frequently labelled 'not genuine' or 'non-trier', but seldom is the defeat of a good youngster attributed to such an unworthy cause. Another consideration is that most two-year-old races are decided over a straight course. Variations in course conformation, which sometimes affect races run over a distance of ground play almost no part in influencing the outcome of pillar-to-post two-year-old sprints. Moreover, the fact that two-year-old races are all over short distances is yet another factor tending towards uniformity. This in turn makes for consistency in the pattern of results. Lastly, juveniles seem to be very little inconvenienced by weight and the small penalties that success attracts in two-year-old non-handicaps seldom have much 'stopping' effect. In short, juveniles are

unquestionably the most reliable medium of investment in racing.

However, even two-year-old form fluctuates and different principles apply at different times of the year.
Here is a month-by-month guide based on patterns of
results that are repeated season after season:

March and April

At the very beginning of the season you should proceed
with great caution. The market is the best guide early
on – the bookmakers' information network is usually a
pretty fair indication of what should happen. Note
particularly two-year-olds which are well-backed first
time out and run well. Nine times out of ten they will be
placed to win within a short time. The combination of
ability, early maturity and fitness, to which the betting
exchanges usually provide the clue, will be exploited by
clever trainers, many of whom specialize in early season coups involving youngsters. After a couple of
weeks, winning form is the most reliable guide. A good
youngster is often capable of running up a sequence of
wins in the opening weeks of the Flat. Conversely, as
the season progresses, do not set too much store by
good spring form. Better-class animals appear on the
scene and the early types, despite having plenty of
experience, are usually overshadowed.

May

This can be difficult month. At the smaller meetings
favourites and well-backed horses do well and are fairly
safe propositions, but at the better class venues caution
must be the watchword. Many races are won by good

youngsters making their first appearance or which ran down the field on their introductory outing. These are animals for which trainers have Epsom and Royal Ascot in mind. They lack the public form of more experienced juveniles which have been on the go since the very early weeks, but their class and superior ability usually tell. Pay particular attention to youngsters from the big 'glamour' stables, especially if well-supported in the ring or the subject of favourable press comment.

June

Here again a distinction must be drawn between the smaller courses and the top-class meetings, particularly the Epsom Derby fixture and Royal Ascot. Form has settled down enough for favourites and near-favourites to go in with pleasing regularity at the less fashionable courses. On the other hand, betting at the big meetings can be something of a lottery – fields are on the large side and form is not always fully exposed.

However, winners and placed horses at these meetings, especially at Ascot, have established themselves in the best available company and should be watched very closely over the summer months. Note also the June meetings at Salisbury. Although not a major venue, it has been used nevertheless for many years by numerous shrewd southern trainers to introduce high-class animals which frequently go on to greater things in the second half of the season.

July

In July, with firm ground and small fields, form at all levels is pretty well exposed. In these circumstances the astute punter can reap a rich harvest. There will be a fair number of hotpots, a few of which will fail at long odds-on. But if you ignore the apparent certainties and shop around among other candidates in reasonably open races at fair prices, you should not find the backing of winners too difficult. Winners and seconds last time out have a high percentage success rate.

August

August ushers in the nursery season and there is also a great increase in the number of races confined to maidens. Both can be a snare and a delusion for backers of well-fancied animals. Stick to good recent form in stakes races which are not for maidens and you should find the going fairly easy.

As far as maiden races are concerned, the form available is often sketchy and sometimes contradictory. My advice is to proceed with great caution or, better still, leave them alone altogether.

Nurseries are handicaps for two-year-olds and as such are always more difficult to weigh up than condition races where weight plays an insignificant part. Although they are sometimes used by gambling stables as the vehicle for well-disguised betting coups, the picture is not all bad — by and large sound form is the best guide to the average nursery. The two-year-old specialist can sometimes spot an outstanding bet at a highly acceptable price, but if you make a habit of betting in nurseries, you are definitely chancing your arm.

September

By September the nursery season is in full swing, and the above remarks on the subject still apply. This month also sees a sequence of high-class meetings – Doncaster, Ayr, Ascot and Newmarket form the climax of the two-year-old season. Now the really top juveniles are on show. Form is reliable, but it is not always the market leaders that succeed. If you look beyond the obvious, you will often find a winner at a good price among the first three or four in the betting. At the smaller meetings form still works out well, but watch for sudden changes in the going due to climatic conditions. They can play havoc with established form.

October and November

Go warily at the back end of the season. The reliability of two-year-old form tends to deteriorate rapidly as the ground becomes heavy and fields get bigger, with many horses running in an attempt to earn their winter keep. If you must back two-year-olds in the last few weeks of the season, make it the exception rather than the rule.

That is a general guide, but how do we isolate the very best two-year-old investments? Well, there is an old racing adage to the effect that you should follow a good youngster until it is beaten. This is clearly sound advice. Once a good two-year-old strikes winning form, it is usually worth watching very closely and many frequently set up sequences of wins. Here then is a good idea: *In two-year-old non-handicaps back any horse which has won its last two outings. If it wins, go on backing it until it is beaten.*

The deceptive simplicity of this method should not disguise its merits. The simple precept of backing all two-year-olds that have recorded at least two consecutive victories produces many, many winners season after season. You may think that qualifiers will always start at very short odds. This is not the case. In fact, although there will obviously be a number of hotpots, many system horses win at decent prices and the majority start at odds-against. In the season which has just ended as I write there were 33 winners from 73 runners with a profit of £40 at £1 level stakes. There were winners at 12-1, 9-1, 7-1 (twice), 11-2, 4-1 and many others at lesser but quite reasonable odds.

This method of backing two-year-olds outlined above is simple but effective. Obviously the level of success will fluctuate from season to season – racing is full of uncertainty – but this is a plan on which you can bet with a reasonable degree of confidence now and in the future.

SYSTEM THREE

Regular investment in handicaps

We nave already seen that favourites are a safer investment in weight-for-age and condition races than in handicaps. This can be amplified into a more general axiom: winners of non-handicap events are easier to find than in races where the handicapper exercises his influence. This is perfectly understandable. The basic idea of a handicap is that each horse is given an equal chance by the allotment of weight according to merit, the better animals carrying heavier burdens than inferior rivals, so that in theory at least every race should result in a dead-heat of all the runners. In these circumstances it is not difficult to understand why handicaps invariably pose greater problems than any other kind of race for the student of form.

Roughly half the races under rules are, however, handicaps. To ignore them completely would lead to an impoverishment to which few backers are prepared to subject themselves. Despite the difficulties, in my opinion there can be sound bets in handicaps, although they will always be more difficult to pinpoint than in any other kind of race.

The assessment of weight carried in previous races, linked to the weight allocated in the race under examination, is the essential clue to the chances of each runner, just as it is the fundamental principle involved in the construction of a handicap in the first place. In other words, the backer who sets out to analyse a handicap is attempting to beat the handicapper at his own game. The starting-point in both operations is a scale that correlates weight carried with distances between runners at the end of a race. Such a scale can of course be applied just as much to non-handicaps as to handicaps, but it is in the latter that it is the basic tool of analysis. There are many versions of this scale, but most racing experts would accept the following as a reasonable compromise between many differing points of view:

Over 5f. or 6f.	1 length – 3 lb
Over 7f.	1 length – 2½ lb
Over 1 mile to 1m.3f.	1 length – 2 lb
Over 1m.4f. to 1m.7f.	1 length – 1½ lb
Over 2 miles or more	1 length – 1 lb

How do we make use of this table? Imagine a race over a mile between, say, Irish Ivy and Clarehaven. Irish Ivy, carrying 9-1, beats Clarehaven by two lengths. Clarehaven's weight is 8-11. On that running, therefore, Irish Ivy is an 8 lb better horse than Clarehaven (9-1 minus 8-11 = 4 lb plus 2 lengths over a mile = $2 \times 2 = 4$ lb = 4 lb plus 4 lb equals 8 lb). When they meet again Irish Ivy carries 9-8, while Clarehaven is set to carry only 8-9. Clarehaven is, therefore, in receipt of 13 lb and since, according to their previous running, Irish Ivy is only 8 lb superior to Clarehaven, the latter should win by a distance equivalent to 5 lb (13 lb minus 8 lb = 5 lb), that is 2½ lengths over a mile.

This is of course a very simple example and if the

analysis of every race were as easy, there would be no difficulty in finding winners and no bookmakers to lay the odds. It is a platitude, however, that horses are not machines capable of analysis by strict mathematical principles. The finishing distance between horses at the end of a race is very much in the hands of the jockeys. It is seldom that a horse is asked to win more easily than necessary, while those behind are often eased once their winning chance has gone. At the same time, horses have their good days and their bad – they do not always run exactly to previous form, far from it. Also, some horses are improving, others deteriorating – very rarely do they maintain a consistent level of ability in the course of their careers or even in the space of one short season.

Moreover, very frequently there are no direct form lines. Then, a guide has to be taken through a third horse which the other two have met at different times. This is known as collateral form and involves comparing the performance of A against C with B against C to arrive at the probable outcome of A against B. The difficulties inherent in this form of comparative assessment multiply in proportion to the number of runners in the race. The business of handicapping soon becomes a very difficult art, involving analysis of direct and collateral form lines, often very tenuous, between horses which are not always running at a consistent standard of form. Yet, by and large, the Jockey Club's professional handicappers do a first-rate job. We hear much of the proverbial 'blot' on the handicap, but it seldom occurs in practice, and in my view, burning the midnight oil looking for it is a waste of time.

The ordinary punter must find easier ways of analysing handicaps. My advice is to forget the study of direct and collateral form built up from the study of dozens of races, which almost invariably leads the amateur to a multiplicity of contradictions, and to concentrate only on very recent form. There is no better guide to a horse's chance, even in a handicap, than how it has performed in its last two or three races. I set out below a list of the most important factors which should be assessed. The framework corresponds roughly to what I have said already about analysing the form of favourites, but this time with particular application to handicaps:

Fitness

I have already said that a horse's fitness is of paramount importance in influencing how it is likely to run. No horse is capable of producing its best form unless it is fully wound up. Unfortunately, horses run at less than peak fitness in handicaps perhaps more often than in any other kind of race. If a trainer is to beat the handicapper, it will often pay him to run a horse in one or even several races when it is short of a gallop or two. The result will be indifferent form and the handicapper will have no alternative but to err on the side of generosity and drop the horse in the weights. When fully fit, the horse can be pulled out to take winning advantage of the easier weight burden it has been assigned. This happens all the time in handicaps, but the astute form student can often detect the process and draw the right conclusion about when a horse is about to do itself full justice.

To some this may seem like sharp practice, but be that as it may, it is part and parcel of the racing game. A more charitable explanation would be to ascribe such variations in running to what are sometimes called 'form waves'. No horse can be kept at its peak all the time – it must be given a break from its exertions, just as men and women need a holiday from their normal working routine. Horses are treated in much the same way. They are gradually brought to a peak, maintain it for a period – a month is about the average, although a lot depends on the individual horse – and then deteriorate pending a rest period, followed by another gradual build-up to top form. The keen form reader can often chart the form cycle of a horse, particularly a handicapper. It is not easy and requires application and patience, but it can be done.

Form

The art of backing handicap winners lies in catching a horse at the peak of its 'form wave'. Of course this is easier said than done, but it is often possible to detect a gradual upward swing in form over two or three races, and then to act accordingly. There will always be handicap winners, more so than in any other kind of race, which defy reasonable analysis, but the most reliable guide remains sound recent form in similar company. Good win and placed form in handicaps of at least roughly equal value, provided it is recent and has not resulted in a dramatic jump in the weights, accounts for many handicap winners. But in accordance with the 'form wave' theory, you should be wary of any horse which has been on the go too long without a break, however impressive its form. Sooner or later it will go over the top.

At the same time a lot of handicaps are won by horses which were unplaced last time out or which have not even shown potential winning form for some time. Such animals are a constant headache to backers. There could be several reasons for the sudden improvement. The obvious one would be a gradual decline in the amount of weight a horse is set to carry as the handicapper responds to repeatedly poor performances by becoming more and more lenient in his assessments. Another explanation is that a horse is readied to win on the training grounds and not on the racecourse. The vital gallop or two which brings a horse right up to its peak takes place not in public, but quietly at home with only the trainer and a few close associates looking on. This type of potential winner is always very difficult to detect. Sometimes the betting market will provide a clue. A horse with little form may shorten rapidly in price before a race. Even if it fails to win, you can be fairly sure that sooner or later the market's confidence will be justified. Again the booking of a top jockey or a smart apprentice can often provide a clue to a sudden upsurge in form. Such portents are not easy to read, but in the end a thorough study of form, even for the most apparently hopeless candidate, is what the backer must rely on.

Strength of the opposition
In theory, every horse in a handicap has an equal chance but weight allocations usually depend on assessments based on many previous races, from which

the handicapper will often form an opinion on the evidence of a horse's very best form. Sometimes there will be a discrepancy between that form, which may be weeks or even months old, and what a horse has achieved very recently. For this reason many handicaps will include runners which can be ignored on the grounds that their current handicap mark is not justified by recent form. In small fields such horses are not difficult to spot and can usually be eliminated. Bigger fields always complicate the picture and it is a sound general principle to confine betting in handicaps to races where runners are not numerous.

Distance

Most horses have an ideal distance, and this is just as true for a handicapper as for any other kind of horse. A horse running at a trip either too short or too far for it will not produce its best form. The probable result will be a revision downwards of the weights, which invariably works to its advantage when put back to its best distance. Again the keen student of form can often draw the right conclusions.

Going

Similarly performances on unsuitable ground will often influence the handicapper to reduce weight burdens in future outings. It is up to the astute punter to spot when ground conditions are right for a particular horse.

An intensive study of all these factors will point the experienced punter in the right direction more often than a complex analysis of direct and collateral form lines stretching back over many weeks or months. However, even then the application of the general principles set out above can still be extremely difficult. What is needed is some rule-of-thumb guide which will direct the backer to those horses worthy of the closest attention. With this in mind I conducted a survey of all handicap races for a recent season. First, I attempted to discover the points in the handicap most productive of winners. Second, I paid particular attention to the position occupied by winners in the betting on a race. For reasons which will become apparent, I confined myself to handicaps with at least ten runners. Here are the results:

HANDICAPS OF TEN OR MORE RUNNERS FOR A COMPLETE SEASON

*Position of winners from
the top weight downwards*

1st, 2nd, 3rd in weights	37% winners
1st, 2nd, 3rd, 4th in weights	48% winners
1st, 2nd, 3rd, 4th, 5th, 6th in weights	62% winners

*Position in betting
of winners*

Favourite, 2nd favourite, 3rd favourite	54% winners
Favourite, 2nd favourite, 3rd favourite, 4th quoted, 5th quoted	75% winners

It is obvious that horses at the top of the handicap are statistically best. Clearly, class tells and particular attention should be focused on the top six weighted horses in any handicap. Again, 75% winners were in the first five in the betting – a very impressive percentage on which to form a basis on which to work. If the two factors are combined, it will enable you to reduce most handicaps to two or three 'possibles' for close analysis along the lines suggested above. Here is an example:

GRAND INQUISITOR	9-3	I WILL	7-2
I WILL	8-11	HIGH PRINCIPLE	5-1
PORTMANTEAU	8-10	GRANI	6-1
SPAHEE	8-6	SPAHEE	6-1
SLAPDASH	8-3	PROMOTION	8-1
PROMOTION	8-0	SHARRAGH	9-1
GRANI	7-13	PORTMANTEAU	10-1
HIGH PRINCIPLE	7-11	SLAPDASH	10-1
WISE FOLLY	7-9	KINSALE	12-1
SHARRAGH	7-9	WISE FOLLY	14-1
PENITENT	7-8	GRAND INQUISITOR	16-1
KINSALE	7-7	PENITENT	20-1

The top six in the weights are:
    GRAND INQUISITOR
    I WILL
    PORTMANTEAU
    SPAHEE
    SLAPDASH
    PROMOTION

The first five in the betting are:
    I WILL

HIGH PRINCIPLE
GRANI
SPAHEE
PROMOTION

Horses common to both groups are:

I WILL
SPAHEE
PROMOTION

In terms of statistical probability, therefore, these three horses are most likely to succeed and it is to them that special attention should be paid.

This kind of analysis will not produce the winner of every race by any means, but it will always enable you to pinpoint the horses with the best chances. It is not infallible, but goes a long way towards isolating the probable winner.

As far as small fields are concerned, I would recommend you to concentrate on the top three, or possibly the top four in the handicap which produce 37% and 48% winners respectively and the first three in the betting (where the winning percentage is 54%). Another example will illustrate the principle:

DELVILLE WOOD	9-8	VIDAUBAN	6-4
LAKE PLACID	9-2	MAHOGANY	5-1
VIDAUBAN	8-9	SNOW LEOPARD	11-2
MAHOGANY	8-2	DELVILLE WOOD	6-1
SNOW LEOPARD	7-13	LAKE PLACID	6-1
PERSIAN ROAD	7-9	VATELLUS	12-1
VATELLUS	7-7	PERSIAN ROAD	20-1

The top four weights are:

DELVILLE WOOD

LAKE PLACID

VIDAUBAN

MAHOGANY

The first three in the betting are:

VIDAUBAN

MAHOGANY

SNOW LEOPARD

Horses common to both groups are:

VIDAUBAN

MAHOGANY

According to our rule-of-thumb test, therefore, one of these two horses should win.

I repeat, the combination of these two factors will not pinpoint every handicap winner, but statistics are on the side of this form of analysis and, allied to the study of form outlined above, the method gives you a fair chance of turning up handicap winners consistently and profitably. To gain some idea of the expected level of success, I conducted a brief survey based on all handicaps, including nurseries, with 12 or more runners during the months of June, July and August of a recent season. It was found that in 47 races out of 105, that is 45%, the winner was one of the first six in the handicap and also one of the first five in the betting. There were seldom more than three 'possibles' in a race thus indicated and the vast majority of winners were in the price range from 5-1 to 10-1.

Regular investment in handicaps is very much a field for the specialist. It is no good betting in handicaps if you have time for little more than a quick glance at the day's runners in the morning paper. But the keen student, with a fair amount of time at his disposal and working along the lines suggested in this chapter, could turn up sound profits with a reasonable degree of regularity. It is not easy, but it is possible.

SYSTEM FOUR

Ways and means
for the season's big handicaps

As we have just seen, handicaps are certainly the most difficult challenge in racing for the backer hoping to make a profit from his investments. This is especially true of the Flat's big handicaps, races like the Lincoln, the Royal Hunt Cup, the Cambridgeshire, etc. Large fields, tangled form lines, good-class horses up against moderate animals, all in with a theoretically equal chance – these and other factors combine to make such events the greatest conundrums that racing has to offer.

As always, good recent form in comparable company should be the basic guide. However, the task of discriminating can be so immensely difficult that there is a lot to be said for departing from orthodox form analysis and instead relying on a system which, if it does not find the winner of every race or even every other race, at least pinpoints enough winners in the course of a season to ensure an annual profit. Remember that given the kind of odds on offer in these events, two or three winners a year will almost certainly produce a handsome credit balance. There follows four such systems – all are based on sound horse sense and all find their fair share of winners, often at quite outrageous odds.

Jockey's mounts

In the normal course of events it is not a paying game to follow indiscriminately the mounts of any jockey, however successful he might be. Top jockeys average 20% winners from the total number of their mounts during a season, yet very, very seldom do they end the year showing a profit at level stakes. In big handicaps, however, the leading jockeys are invariably associated with live candidates and between them they usually capture a significant number of these races in the course of a season. The following system has a very healthy record over the years and is well worth a trial:

In the big Flat handicaps concentrate on the mounts of the six leading jockeys for the season. Take the two horses so indicated which are allotted the lowest weights.

Most newspapers feature up-to-date information on the riders who are currently leading in the race for the jockeys' championship. It is simply a matter of discovering the leading six at any given time and taking the two riding at the lowest weights. At the beginning of the season, for races like the Lincoln and the big spring handicaps, a more reliable guide is certainly the six leading jockeys of the previous season, because early on, no clear order of merit will have been established.

This method will not pinpoint the winner of every big handicap, but usually finds several winners during the year. A big race sequence of the forty or so most competitive handicaps is ideal for the plan, and a handful of winners should produce a sound profit.

Following the five-year-olds

I have always been impressed by the number of older horses that run well in big handicaps. In fact, not many horses are kept in training beyond the age of four. There is a good reason for this: most horses begin to deteriorate for racing purposes after they reach their physical peak at that age. Some, however, do not. The clever trainer can always spot handicappers good enough to pay their way at five. They are outnumbered by four-year-olds in the ratio of approximately 4-1, yet the record of senior horses in big handicaps is very good indeed. Recently I conducted a survey based on their performance in the Flat's top ten handicaps over a five-year period. From 206 runners there were 18 winners which produced a level stake profit of 69 points. Obviously bulk betting on every five-year-old runner will not appeal to the majority, but the lesson is clear. You would do well to study very closely the chances of all five-year-olds in these races. Two or three against the field will often succeed where more orthodox methods usually fail.

Drop in the weights

Handicapping is a very difficult art. It is largely a matter of opinion and within a maximum weight range of three stones, a difference of a couple of pounds more or less between horses of similar class seldom makes much difference to the result. It is a fact, however, that horses invariably appreciate a sudden large drop in weight from the burdens they are accustomed to carrying. At the top of the weights in valuable handicaps there are invariably a few horses whose class and ability

38

entitle them to carry hefty imposts. Horses further down the handicap frequently benefit because they are sharply down-graded in terms of the weight they are usually asked to shoulder. Here then is a sound plan:

Compare the weight a horse is set to carry in the race under review, ignoring apprentice allowances, with the weight actually carried on its immediately previous run in a handicap. If there is a horse now set to carry at least 10 lb less than last time, back it.

To the form purist this simple idea may seem extremely unscientific, but the fact remains that many big handicaps are won by horses which satisfy the basic system rule. The intelligent application of this precept can pinpoint some really fine big-race winners.

Form horse

Few big handicaps are won by the favourite, and second favourites do little better. Statistics show that apart from the occasional screaming outsider, most of these races go to a relatively small group from the third in the betting upwards. Anyone seeking a sporting bet and who is prepared to take a calculated risk might try the following plan:

1: Assess the third, fourth, fifth, sixth, seventh and eighth horses in the betting. If necessary, use a reliable betting forecast.
2: Assess the chance of each horse on the basis of the following scale:

LAST TIME OUT		TWO PREVIOUS OUTINGS	
WON	5 points	WON	3 points
2nd	3 points	2nd	2 points
3rd	2 points	3rd	1 point
4th	1 point	4th	Nil

3: The horse with the highest resultant rating is the selection for the race.

Here is an example of the method in operation:

	KISAKI	5-1	Favourite
	BLUEFIN	7-1	2nd Favourite
200	GERMANICUS	9-1	2+0+0=2 points
001	DRAGON FLY	11-1	0+0+5=5 points
241	GOLD MIST	12-1	2+0+5=7 points
210	PARAMOUNT	12-1	2+3+0=5 points
402	DACIAN	14-1	0+0+3=3 points
310	PINCHED	16-1	1+3+0=4 points

GOLD MIST with 7 points is the selection.

There is no easy solution to the problem of the Flat's big handicaps. Each of the above approaches is basically sound, however, and has achieved a fair degree of success in the past. With their aid, big handicaps need not be too difficult.

Each-way betting
I think it is fair to say that most punters opt to bet each-way in races with large fields and open betting. Hence the popularity of each-way betting in big handicaps. As a general policy, however, this approach is wrong and a little simple mathematics will demonstrate the reason why. Let us examine a race with, say, 21 runners. The true odds against any horse winning are 20-1 and the true odds against any one finishing in the first three are 18-3 or 6-1. The bookmaker on the other hand would offer one-fifth the odds for a place,

that is, only 4-1, which is a full two points under the real mathematical chance.

In fact, the smaller the field, the nearer the book-maker's odds for a place correspond to the true odds. This becomes clear if we examine a race with only eight runners, the minimum permitted for each-way betting. The true odds against any horse winning are 7-1 and for a place 5-3. The bookmaker would offer 7-5 against a horse finishing in the first three, which is only marginally worse than the true odds.

Thus it becomes apparent that each-way betting is in fact a better proposition in small fields, provided of course a fair price is on offer about your fancy. As far as big handicaps are concerned, in terms of value calculated along mathematical lines, two separate one-point bets for a win are superior to staking one point each-way on only one horse. The best way to tackle these races, therefore, is to take a small number against the field to win. Each-way betting, even with the place concessions in these events which are offered by some bookmakers, represents poor value.

SYSTEM FIVE

Profitable pointers from the Classics

The five Classic races for three-year-olds – the 2000 and 1000 Guineas run at Newmarket in the spring, the Derby and Oaks at Epsom and the St. Leger at Doncaster towards the end of the season – are the showpieces of British racing. These events are never easy to analyse and to the 'systemite' their chief value lies in the clues they provide for the future.

After all, they are contested by the very cream of the three-year-old generation. It would be curious indeed if they did not furnish the alert punter with profitable pointers for the rest of the season. In my view, and this is borne out by a prolonged study of statistics, the first six home in each race are the ones on which to focus special attention. Winners and seconds, however, should be ignored most years – horses are not machines and are quite capable of being beaten in subsequent runs despite their moment of Classic glory and despite the very short odds they automatically attract as a result.

The records show, however, that horses which finished third, fourth, fifth and sixth are well worth listing and following in their subsequent outings. The St. Leger comes too late in the season to be of much value and the horses to follow are drawn from the first four big races only.

The system rules are:

1: List the third, fourth, fifth and sixth in the first four Classics, the 2000 Guineas, the 1000 Guineas, the Derby and the Oaks.

2: Follow qualifiers on their next four outings in this country. After four races they are deleted from the list.

This system in miniature has a good record over the years. Here are the results for a recent twelve-year period at £1 level stakes:

£40 profit	from 36 bets
£16 profit	from 39 bets
£9 profit	from 39 bets
£14 profit	from 29 bets
£1 loss	from 28 bets
£12 profit	from 28 bets
£5 profit	from 31 bets
£5 loss	from 28 bets
£1 loss	from 39 bets
£22 profit	from 44 bets
£16 profit	from 19 bets
£4 profit	from 50 bets

Although the system is clearly not the road to an overnight fortune, in a good year you can expect 50% profit on outlay and from the evidence of the twelve years' results examined, a substantial loss is virtually precluded. You are automatically on some of the best horses of the year and if the rewards are not staggering, they can still be very acceptable.

SYSTEMS FOR THE JUMPS

SYSTEM SIX

How to back favourites over the jumps

Until the early Sixties National Hunt racing was very much the poor relation of the Flat — horses raced for small prizes and fields were seldom competitive. In these circumstances winter favourites returned very high winning percentages, so much so that few backers looked beyond market-leaders when making their selections. Now the situation has changed. Television has contributed immeasurably to the popularization of the jumping game and sponsorship has increased the level of prize money to such an extent that it begins to approach the financial rewards that the Flat has always offered. The result has been that more and more owners have come into the sport. With the consequent involvement of a far greater number of horses of better class and more intensive competition, favourites no longer retain this stranglehold over winter racing that they once did.

Nevertheless, returns for favourites in certain kinds of races and at certain courses are still extremely consistent. Nothing is certain in racing, but a policy of discrimination could produce a reasonable margin of profit for the patient backer. The first step is to analyse the winter favourite picture as a whole. Below is the record for a recent five-year period:

Non-handicap hurdles	45%
Handicap hurdles	32%
Chases of 3 miles or more (non-handicaps)	40%
Chases of 3 miles or more (handicaps)	30%
Under 3 mile Chases (non-handicaps)	38%
Under 3 mile Chases (handicaps)	35%
ALL RACES	37%

The overall situation is remarkably similar to the Flat. In particular, returns for non-handicaps are clearly superior to those for handicaps. Two types of race stand out: non-handicap hurdles with a winning percentage of 45% and long distance non-handicap chases with 40%.

As is the case with the Flat, the basic percentage can be improved by studying the returns for different tracks. Here is a breakdown showing the best courses for non-handicap hurdle favourites over the five-year period:

FAVOURITES IN NON-HANDICAP HURDLES

1.	TOWCESTER	62%
2.	UTTOXETER	56%
3.	WINDSOR	48%
4.	CARLISLE	46%
5.	FOLKESTONE	45%
6.	LINGFIELD	45%

7. WETHERBY   44%
8. DONCASTER   43%
9. MARKET RASEN   43%
10. SANDOWN   43%
11. WARWICK   43%
12. WOLVERHAMPTON   43%

These figures include returns from novice hurdles about which many racing experts are extremely cautious. Certainly there can be surprising results in this kind of race – inexperienced horses with little form in the book are not always the most reliable investments. On the other hand, it is not difficult to spot a good novice hurdler and the racecourse market has a habit of getting these races right. An intensive analysis revealed that a large number of winning favourites in novice hurdles are winners or seconds last time out. I would not go so far as to say that everything else should be ignored, but it will certainly pay to concentrate on those favourites which either won or finished second on their previous outing.

As far as non-handicap steeplechases of three miles or more are concerned, prospects are even brighter for certain courses where some very high winning percentages are recorded:

FAVOURITES IN
NON-HANDICAP CHASES
OF 3 MILES OR MORE

1. KELSO   60%
2. HAYDOCK   57%
3. ASCOT   56%

4.	TAUNTON	52%
5.	AYR	51%
6.	KEMPTON	51%
7.	DEVON AND EXETER	50%
8.	SANDOWN	50%
9.	WORCESTER	50%
10.	CATTERICK	49%
11.	SEDGEFIELD	49%
12.	WINDSOR	49%

There are not a great many races of this type in the course of a season and the number is cut still further by concentrating on the top dozen courses for favourites, but it is clear that returns are exceptionally good. Moreover, starting prices are usually quite reasonable – the 49–60% winning rates do not stem from strings of odds-on chances. In short, this type of favourite is a very sound proposition indeed.

The winning favourite percentages for both non-handicap hurdles and long-distance non-handicap chases are so good that it could be argued that further discrimination is unnecessary. However, I am convinced that if you apply the same kind of form criteria to these races as were recommended for Flat favourites, the position can be improved even more. These criteria are similar to those laid down earlier:

1: Before having a bet, satisfy yourself that a horse is fully fit.

2: Favourites should have public form in similar company which suggests they are capable of fulfilling market expectations. We have already seen that novice hurdlers first or second last time out do best.

Much the same applies to senior hurdlers. As for chasers, win or placed form on recent outings gives extra grounds for confidence. Beware of horses which have a tendency to fall – a glance at six-figure form will reveal those which are not certain to put in a clear round.

3: As with Flat races, favourites opposed by a good number of horses which have consistent win and placed form should be treated with caution.

4: Obviously there are distance specialists over the jumps just as much as on the Flat, but most jumpers are either two- or three-mile horses and distance preferences are neither so marked nor so important.

Similarly the going is much less important in the winter branch of the sport. Ground conditions usually vary between good and heavy. Most jumpers regularly perform on the same kind of surface and with a few exceptions are not nearly so fastidious as their Flat counterparts. Beware, however, the firm ground which sometimes comes with spring – it can make nonsense of months of form on softish ground.

Although not the force they once were, jumping favourites still show remarkably consistent returns provided you exercise discrimination. Certainly the position is still much less difficult than on the Flat. Allied to proper staking, favourites can be made to pay, given patience and the slice of luck without which no racing venture can succeed.

SYSTEM SEVEN

A winning combination for favourites and outsiders

The system outlined below is ideal for anyone who is actually having a day at the races or who has an afternoon to spend in a betting shop. Confirmed favourite-backers will find a means of enhancing profits by thoughtful investment on outsiders. Those who prefer longshots will be able to pay for their tilt at the book by cash gained from bets on winning favourites.

The basic idea behind the method is to use stakes won from a source which provides a high percentage of short-priced winners to finance bets on lucrative propositions at longer odds. The figure I refer to can be as high as 70% and can be achieved in the following way:

By backing the first and sixth race favourites at jumping meetings, the punter may find at least one winner 70% of the time.

Obviously this is a highly significant piece of statistical fact if it can be harnessed to a well-conceived programme of betting. The following set of rules is, I believe, just such a programme:

1: Bet only in the first, third and sixth races on the card at National Hunt meetings.
2: Stake one point on the favourite in the first race.
3: If the favourite is successful in the first race, stake

half a point to win each on the third, fourth and fifth quoted horses in the third race. Selections are determined by examining the racecourse market or the betting shop prices 'show' just before the 'off'. Win or lose, there is no bet in the sixth race.

4: If the favourite is beaten in the first race, there is no bet in the third race, but a stake of one point on the favourite in the sixth race.

Here are two examples of the system in operation. In the first the favourite won the opener:

FIRST RACE	1 point	Favourite	won 5-2	Profit 2½ points
THIRD RACE		Favourite	5-2	
		2nd Favourite	100-30	
	½ point	3rd Favourite	6-1	Loss ½ point
	½ point	4th Quoted	15-2	Loss ½ point
	½ point	5th Quoted	won 8-1	Profit 4 points

Total Profit 5½ points

SIXTH RACE		No bet

Now an example where the favourite is beaten in the first race:

FIRST RACE	1 point	Favourite	lost	Loss 1 point
THIRD RACE		No bet		
SIXTH RACE	1 point	Favourite	won 9-4	Profit 2¼ points

Total Profit 1¼ points

In both examples things worked out very well and it would be wrong to expect similar success every time.

However, the principles of the method are fundamentally sound. If the favourite wins the first race, you have a free tilt on good-priced horses in the third, almost always a handicap where, statistically, horses at decent odds have the best chance and first and second favourites have a poor record. If the favourite loses in the first race, you forgo a bet in the third and concentrate on the recovery of lost stakes by betting on the favourite in the last race. Remember that my statistics for jumping meetings show that the first and sixth races, usually both non-handicaps, are the best for favourites. In terms of favourites, therefore, you may succeed 70% of the time. The system really comes good when the favourite wins the first and puts cash in your hands for a winning bet at a good price in the third race.

This method offers a sporting chance of a winning day at any winter meeting. Profits will never be spectacular and losing days will certainly occur, but as an occasional bet it has a great deal in its favour.

SYSTEM EIGHT

Speculative jumping wagers

So far we have dealt with systems for National Hunt racing which concentrate wholly or in part on favourites. But just as the Flat offers sound opportunities for punters who prefer a more speculative form of betting, so there are plenty of chances for jumping enthusiasts who are prepared to take a calculated risk. There is nothing infallible about the three methods that follow, but each is based on sound racing principles and each has shown a degree of consistency in the past which justifies its inclusion in this book.

Betting in handicap chases

On the face of it, horses which are continually asked to jump stiff fences over two miles or more are not a sound betting proposition. However, most of the horses which have graduated to handicap chases and run regularly over the bigger obstacles are seasoned campaigners which have learned their trade the hard way. No horse likes falling and a good chaser soon learns how to take care of itself in a race. Yet there are exceptions. Races like the Grand National, for instance, where huge fences, a crowded field and a long, tiring distance cause many falls, are best forgotten. In the main, however, a good-class chaser, even though it is running in a handicap, is a fairly reliable medium of investment. The difficulty of course is to sort out the right chasers to back.

Above all we must look for consistency. In any kind of race the consistent horse offers the best chance of a profit in the long run. In fact, horses well to the fore in the betting virtually monopolize these events, and in the following method we do not look too far beyond the obvious. Here are the suggested rules:

1: Bet only in handicap steeplechases of seven or more runners.
2: Consider only the first four quoted in the betting forecast of a reliable newspaper.
3: Assess each horse's last three outings by means of the following scale:

LAST TIME OUT		TWO PREVIOUS OUTINGS	
WON	5 points	WON	3 points
2nd	3 points	2nd	2 points
3rd	2 points	3rd	1 point
4th	1 point		

Failure to complete the course one or more times in the last three runs (e.g. fell, brought down, unseated rider, pulled up, etc.): deduct 1 point from the total.
4: The horse with the highest points total is the selection for the race.

An example will make the working of the method clear:

56

HANDICAP CHASE 11 runners

402	SOLFORD	$0+0+3 =$	3 points
2F2	OUR HOPE	$2-1+3 =$	4 points
110	AFRICANA	$3+3+0 =$	6 points
213	SENECA	$2+3+2 =$	7 points

SENECA with 7 points is the selection

There will certainly be losing runs with this method, but it will also produce good winners. Prices can be anything up to around 8-1, so there is every chance of a profit for the system given a fair trial.

Betting in handicap hurdles

Handicap hurdlers are certainly not as consistent as their chasing counterparts, despite the fact that the obstacles are much easier. The probable explanation is that, while comparatively few horses are good enough to make the grade in chasing company, almost any horse can be schooled for hurdles and, given a certain racing ability, can win a handicap off the right weight. Approaching the problem in statistical terms, here is an analysis of winning handicap hurdle weights for a complete season. Here the 12-7 to 10-0 weight range is broken down into six equal parts:

12-7 —12-2	2%
12-1 —11-10	5%
11-9 —11-4	12%
11-3 —10-12	22%
10-11—10-6	28%
10-5 or less	31%

The extent of the tendency for winners to be concentrated at the bottom end of the handicap is surprising, but perhaps bears out what I said earlier: there are many opportunities for well-schooled animals to get into such races on a handy mark in terms of weight, to the disadvantage of better class horses which often find themselves 'anchored' by stiff burdens.

Here are the suggested rules for the method I have in mind:

1: Bet only in handicap hurdles.
2: Back any horse which won last time out and is carrying (inclusive of any weight allowance for its rider) 10-6 or less.

There will not be too many qualifiers with this idea. Losing runs will certainly occur, but winners can start at very good prices indeed. It is not an idea to put your proverbial shirt on, but for an occasional bet on a live candidate, there is a lot to be said for it.

A plan for Saturdays

The following method is specially designed for those who like to do most of their betting at the weekends when there is plenty of racing, but it is workable any day when there are three or more meetings. It is a percentage system, based on a predictable pattern of results in relation to the structure of betting markets rather than on the orthodox study of form. Here is a summary of the idea:

1: Bet only when there are at least three meetings on any one day.
2: Bet in all races where the favourite is priced at 5-2 or more in a reliable betting forcast.
3: In each qualifying race back the third and fourth quoted horses in the forecast.
4: Bet at level stakes on all qualifiers.

What this amounts to is backing likely alternatives to relatively weak favourites. With plenty of qualifiers, there is a fair chance of finding enough winners at decent prices to offset an outlay which is larger than usual. Here is an example taken from a typical Saturday in November during a recent season:

	3rd Favourite	4th Quoted
Favourite 100-30	Lost 5-1	Won 7-1
Favourite 100-30	Lost 9-2	Lost 11-2
Favourite 3-1	Lost 6-1	Won 11-1
Favourite 4-1	Lost 5-1	Lost 5-1
Favourite 9-2	Won 5-1	Lost 5-1
Favourite 5-2	Lost 11-2	Lost 7-1
Favourite 100-30	Lost 6-1	Lost 7-1

OUTLAY   14 points
RETURN   7+1+11+1+5+ 1 = 26 points
PROFIT   12 points

Obviously there will be losing days with this method, but for anyone who likes to have plenty of eggs in his basket, the idea has definite potential.

Betting systems can only do so much. You need luck, however well-conceived the plan, but the three set out above, though speculative, are based on sound betting principles and have a good record. For the backer blessed with a little patience, they can all be thoroughly recommended.

SYSTEMS FOR FLAT
AND JUMPS

SYSTEM NINE
How to spread the risk under both codes

The old-time professional backers regularly supported several horses in the same race so that a profit was guaranteed whichever horse in the selected group was successful. This kind of betting requires considerable capital, a lightning facility with odds and a willingness to bet at odds-on more often than not. There is little appeal for the average punter in this style of operating and the imposition of betting tax has made it even less attractive.

However, there is one variant of the principle of multiple betting which can be used to considerably reduce the chance of loss and of which all serious backers should be aware. Suppose you find a horse which you think has a clear chance of winning. You decide to back it. But there are always dangers to your selection – that is what racing is all about. Suppose you can isolate the main danger. There is a simple formula which allows you to make a substantial investment on the principal selection and at the same time a second bet on the 'danger' which will retrieve the whole of the stake if successful. The formula is as follows:

First determine your total outlay on the race. Add one point to the price of the danger and divide into the total outlay. The

63

answer is the stake to be placed on the danger. This is deducted from the total outlay to give the stake on the principal selection.

Here is an example:

INTENDED OUTLAY: £10

DANGER: price say 9-1
         stake 9+1=10 into £10=£1

PRINCIPAL SELECTION: price say 3-1
                stake £10 minus £1=£9

RETURN AND PROFIT

If the danger wins, £1 at 9-1 returns £10 (£1 at 9-1=£9 plus £1 stake=£10); the whole of the original outlay is thus saved.

If the principal selection wins, £9 at 3-1 returns £36 (£9 at 3-1=£27 plus £9 stake=£36); the profit is thus £26 (total return £36 minus total £10 outlay on the two selections=£26).

To make my meaning absolutely clear, here is another example where the principal selection is 4-1 and the danger is 12-1:

INTENDED OUTLAY: £10

DANGER: price 12-1
        stake 12+1=13 into £10=£0.77

PRINCIPAL SELECTION: price 4-1
                stake £10 minus
                £0.77=£9.23

RETURN AND PROFIT:

If the danger wins, £0.77 at 12-1 returns £10.01 (£0.77 at 12-1=£9.24 plus £0.77=£10.01); the whole of the original outlay is thus saved.

If the principal selection wins, £9.23 at 4-1 returns £46.15 (£9.23 at 4-1= £36.92 plus £9.23 stake= £46.15); the profit is thus £36.15 (total return £46.15 minus total £10 outlay on the two selections= £36.15).

Bookmakers dislike stakes involving odd amounts in pence. In the above example, therefore, it would be desirable to adjust stakes so that £0.75 is invested on the danger and £9.25 is placed on the principal selection. This does not destroy the mathematical symmetry of the staking and the difference in the return on the danger or the profit on the main selection is similarly a matter of a few pence.

The formula works very well indeed provided that the danger selection is at a fairly good price. If, however, the danger is a favourite or near-favourite, it is advisable to abandon the formula, particularly when its price is so short (that is, odds-on) that the required stake is larger than for the principal selection.

The formula can be readily adapted to allow for two danger selections, for example:

INTENDED OUTLAY: £10
FIRST DANGER: price say 7-1
                stake 7+1=8 into £10= £1.25
SECOND DANGER: price say 9-1
                stake 9+1= 10 into £10= £1
PRINCIPAL SELECTION: price say 3-1
                     stake £10 minus £1.25
                     minus £1= £7.75

RETURNS AND PROFIT:

If the first danger wins, £1.25 at 7-1 returns £10 (£1.25 at 7-1=£8.75 plus £1.25 stake=£10); the whole of the original outlay is thus saved.

If the second danger wins, £1 at 9-1 returns £10 (£1 at 9-1=£9 plus £1 stake=£10); the whole of the original outlay is thus saved.

If the principal selection wins, £7.75 at 3-1 returns £31 (£7.75 at 3-1=£23.25 plus £7.75 stake=£31); the profit is thus £21 (total return £31 minus total £10 outlay on the three selections=£21).

It is even more necessary here than when using a single danger to make sure that subsidiary selections are not at prohibitive odds.

This formula can only be operated with maximum efficiency on the course or in a betting shop where actual prices are known and exact calculations can be made. However, if you use a betting forecast, the principle involved is still sound enough, except when there is a complete revision of preconceived ideas in the actual market on the race.

Thus, for a small sacrifice in overall profit, this formula goes a long way to insuring against the striking of losing bets. *This applies particularly to handicaps* where one horse seldom stands out and prices are on the whole good. However, whatever the kind of race, the formula can be used to launch an assault on the bookmaker with striking results in the backer's favour.

SYSTEM TEN

An economical racing perm with high profit potential

Perms are commonplace in pools and fixed-odds betting on football, but much less so in racing. In many ways this is a pity for a racing permutation can be the road to a big win for a comparatively small outlay. The nearest everyday approach in the racing world is that old favourite, the Yankee – four selections backed in six doubles, four trebles and an accumulator. The permutation presented here is, I believe, much superior. It costs the same and offers the same kind of opportunity to land multiple doubles, trebles and an accumulator, yet covers more selections, which can only mean more chances to win.

Set out in its football-type format, the permutation looks like this:

```
1.   X              X X X   X
2.   X X                  X X X
3.     X X        X X          X
4.       X X            X X   X
5.         X X X          X X
6.         X   X X X X
```

Bookmakers are always suspicious of this kind of thing, especially the smaller ones, so it is better to write out the bet in full. Suppose we make our six selections as follows:

1. Monte Christo
2. Fox Covert
3. Alistair
4. Arbutus
5. Purple Sand
6. Chivalry

There is nothing special in the setting out of the 1 to 6 order, but once decided upon, it must be adhered to throughout when writing down the bet in full. The complete list of bets would look like this:

DOUBLES

Monte Christo
Fox Covert

Fox Covert
Alistair

Alistair
Arbutus

Arbutus
Purple Sand

Purple Sand
Chivalry

TREBLES

Monte Christo
Alistair
Purple Sand

Monte Christo
Alistair
Chivalry

Monte Christo
Arbutus
Chivalry

Fox Covert
Arbutus
Chivalry

ACCUMULATORS

Monte Christo
Fox Covert
Purple Sand
Chivalry

Fox Covert
Alistair
Arbutus
Purple Sand

In my view the guarantees are quite remarkable:

2 WINNERS

2-1 against a winning double.

3 WINNERS

Either a double *OR* 2 doubles *OR* a treble.

4 WINNERS

Either 2 doubles *OR* 3 doubles *OR* 2 doubles and a treble *OR* a double and 2 trebles *OR* 2 doubles and an accumulator *OR* 3 doubles and an accumulator.

5 WINNERS

Either 3 doubles and 3 trebles *OR* 4 doubles, a treble and an accumulator *OR* 3 doubles, 2 trebles and an accumulator.

6 WINNERS

THE JACKPOT!

The permutation can be operated on any racing day, but several meetings offer more chance to exercise discrimination in the choice of selections. Try to make a balanced list of horses in terms of likely starting prices — two short-priced favourites, two in the 3-1 to 4-1 range, and a couple at longer odds without including screaming outsiders in the 'no-hoper' category, would be my own idea of a good combination.

Remember that with six winners, even at quite modest odds, the potential profit is enormous, so that it is always best to place the bet with a 'no limit' bookmaker. Many smaller bookmakers impose limits which are easily exceeded by winning multiple bets of this kind.

At only eleven bets a go, and given the excellent guarantees, this racing permutation is one of the best of its kind.

SYSTEM ELEVEN

An automatic way
to winning doubles for
Flat or Jumps

We have already noted in an earlier chapter the consistency of first- and last-race favourites at jumping meetings. The picture is much the same as far as the Flat is concerned. Usually non-handicaps, both races have a healthy winning percentage for favourites. The situation in regard to the second race on the card is less favourable, although there are seasons when the returns for favourites are very good indeed, particularly in the winter. Viewed as a whole, however, a multiple wager based on doubles in these three events can be the road to steady, if unspectacular, profits.

The idea is to bet only when there are at least three meetings, that is always on a Saturday, and sometimes during the week. The following layout guarantees a winning double provided at least one favourite from each meeting obliges. At the same time multiple coups are possible and indeed probable when the gods smile.

The basic format on which the bet is based is as follows:

    1st race Meeting A.
    1st race Meeting B
    1st race Meeting C
    _____

2nd race Meeting A
2nd race Meeting B
2nd race Meeting C

1st race Meeting A
6th race Meeting B
6th race Meeting C

6th race Meeting A
1st race Meeting B
6th race Meeting C

6th race Meeting A
6th race Meeting B
1st race Meeting C

When writing out the bet, we first set down the races and times as follows:

Ascot 12-15
Ascot 12-55 (Meeting A)
Ascot 3-0

Catterick 12-30
Catterick 1-0 (Meeting B)
Catterick 3-0

Leicester 1-15
Leicester 1-45 (Meeting C)
Leicester 3-45

Applying the basic format set out earlier, we arrive at the final version of the bet:

Fav. 12-15 Ascot
Fav. 12-30 Catterick
Fav. 1-15 Leicester

Fav. 12-55 Ascot
Fav. 1-0 Catterick
Fav. 1-45 Leicester

Fav. 12-15 Ascot
Fav. 3-0 Catterick
Fav. 3-45 Leicester

Fav. 3-0 Ascot
Fav. 12-30 Catterick
Fav. 3-45 Leicester

Fav. 3-0 Ascot
Fav. 3-0 Catterick
Fav. 1-15 Leicester

Checking is simple: two successful favourites in any group must mean a winning double. On occasion three favourites will win in the same group, which gives three successful doubles. The more winners in the nine races, the greater the number of winning doubles, but the basic guarantee remains cast-iron: one winning favourite at each of the three meetings must turn up a successful double. It is of course perfectly possible to win with only two winners from the nine races covered.

A check on a few weeks' results will show that it is very seldom that the whole fifteen-point stake is lost; that is, you fail to get at least one double up. Many weeks you could land multiple winning doubles. Of course a lot depends on prices as well as the number of successful favourites, but if you are prepared to stick with this plan, preferably ploughing back profits from winnings, you have a fighting chance of relieving the bookmaker of some of his cash.

The method as outlined above is fully automatic and always operates on the first, second and sixth races on the card at each meeting. It would be perfectly acceptable, however, for the punter to choose his own races on which to apply the formula. Using the principles and criteria set out in earlier chapters on favourites, it might well be possible to improve upon the overall percentage of winners. At one meeting you might decide that the first, fourth and fifth races are more likely to produce more winners than rigid adherence to the first, second and sixth race pattern I have suggested. At another venue the second, fifth and sixth races may seem to offer the best potential, and so on.

Modification of the formula to allow for exercise of judgement in this way is not difficult. Suppose you decide to operate on the following patterns at the three chosen meetings:

MEETING A
second race
third race
sixth race

MEETING B
first race
fourth race
fifth race

MEETING C
third race
fourth race
sixth race

To work out the correct rota of doubles apply this general formula:

GROUPS OF THREE
(reading downwards)

Cover each group
for 3 doubles
= 15 bets

	1	–	1	–	–
Meeting A	–	2	–	–	–
	–	–	–	3	3
	1	–	–	1	–
Meeting B	–	2	–	–	–
	–	–	3	–	3
	1	–	–	–	1
Meeting C	–	2	–	–	–
	–	–	3	3	–

At Meeting A 1 is the second race, 2 is the third race and 3 is the sixth race. At Meeting B 1 is the first, 2 is the fourth and 3 is the fifth race. At Meeting C 1 is the third on the card, 2 is the fourth and 3 is the sixth. So the five groups to cover for three doubles become:

Meeting A	2nd race	3rd race	2nd race	6th race	6th race
Meeting B	1st race	4th race	5th race	1st race	5th race
Meeting C	3rd race	4th race	6th race	6th race	3rd race
	3 doubles	3 doubles	3 doubles	3 doubles	3 doubles

In writing out the bet, it would be necessary to specify actual times of the races and add the instructions in exactly the same way as already illustrated for the fully automatic version of the formula. The guarantees remain unchanged.

Whether you decide to plug away at the first, second and sixth race pattern each week or to vary the races according to judgement and circumstances is very much a matter for individual temperament. But either way the general formula has immense potential, given the fact that between two and three winning favourites per meeting is the statistical probability. Statistics in racing can only do so much of course, but as a regular investment this method certainly represents sound business.

SYSTEM TWELVE

Getting the best out of the racing press

Nowadays the racing enthusiast is better served by the press than ever before. Racing is the only sport which has two specialist daily newspapers devoted to it and the British sporting press is the equal of any in the world. Also, the racing pages of the daily papers contain a vast amount of information – full details of runners and riders, form figures and ratings, betting forecasts, brief form summaries, experts' selections and much more is condensed into highly readable form for a few pence. Newspapers are a vital part of the racing enthusiast's equipment.

How you make use of the information presented on the racing pages is of course a matter of individual preference, but here I would like to deal particularly with the selections of press experts. Racing correspondents are highly paid professionals whose livelihood depends on their success at picking winners. With more expertise and more time for study at their disposal than the average punter, it seems reasonable to suppose that their tips should be a rich source of winners. Selections can be divided into two broad categories: naps – the horse each expert regards as the day's best bet – and in the case of the big names, blanket coverage of the day's racing in the form of a selection for every race.

On the face of it, the nap selection of any successful

pressman ought to be a gilt-edged proposition. Sadly, this is not the case. In fact, only one correspondent in four shows a seasonal profit at level stakes on his naps. This is disappointing to say the least and underlines just how difficult is the racing game. Moreover, the losing runs on nap selections can be terrifying. Only rarely does a napster, even one who manages to finish the season with a profit, keep a double-figure losing run off his record for the year. Runs of 15–20 losing selections are commonplace and occasionally extend to close on 30. Moreover, the same correspondent can do exceptionally well one year, only to end up with a huge deficit the next. In short, naps are inconsistent and risky propositions as a vehicle for serious investment. I have experimented with naps from many angles over the years and have no hesitation in saying that I know of no way in which they can be made to pay as a regular form of investment.

As far as the race-by-race selections of these experts are concerned, there are two lines of approach: relying on indications which follow from a consensus of expert opinion and concentrating on the selections of a single correspondent.

When there is a consensus of opinion among experts about the outcome of a particular race, you would expect to have special grounds for confidence. This can often be misplaced. A consensus of opinion usually points to the favourite and as we have seen, favourites fail quite regularly. As for open contests where selections take a wide range, one expert or a small group of them will find the winner, but many others will fail to do so. The backer is left to decide which set of views is likely to prove the correct one. The most one can say is that if you have good grounds for choosing a particular horse to back, you can bet with extra confidence if a significant group of experts endorse your choice. Beyond that I would not care to go.

As for the race-by-race selections of a single expert, there are winners and losers, short-priced selections and outsiders and, make no mistake, a certain hefty deficit over a reasonable period of level-stake betting. However, some tips are better than others. Which? To find out I conducted a survey based on the selections of one of our leading press experts, a racing journalist of national renown with a record of consistent success over many years. A season of Flat selections, and one of National Hunt, were put under the statistical microscope in the hope of finding a pattern of results which would be to the discriminating backer's advantage.

The first line of approach was to examine the price at which selections started. Do short-priced tips do better than those at longer odds? What is the best price range on which to concentrate? How do outsiders fare? The answers to these and other questions can be found in the following summary:

Odds-on	49%	winners
Evens to 9-4	21%	winners
5-2 to 4-1	23%	winners
9-2 to 8-1	6%	winners
17-2 or more	8%	winners
ALL SELECTIONS	23%	winners

As you might expect, odds-on selections did best in terms of winning percentage, although a surprising number were beaten. Remember, moreover, that this covers all rates from 10-11 downwards. Clearly, with the high rate of taxation that prevails, there is not much future in this type of selection.

The largest number of selections fell within the range from evens to 9-4 inclusive, but the percentage was slightly inferior to the next category, namely from 5-2 to 4-1. It does not require a mathematical genius to see that the greatest potential lies in this group.

Before moving on to other factors, I should say a word about the longer-priced selections. A surprising number started between 9-2 and 8-1 and in fact recorded a substantial level-stake loss. Avoid them — that is the obvious conclusion. The outsider category did not do too badly when viewed over the whole length of the survey. The incidence of winners was not high at 8%, but at the kind of prices returned, it often pays to row in when a seasoned expert is prepared to publicly chance his arm. After all he must have a good reason for making the selection in the first place and if you are looking for a big-priced winner, perhaps as a profit-booster for doubles, trebles, etc., you could do a lot worse.

The next stage was to analyse where selections were placed last time out. Here is the result:

LAST TIME OUT

Won	39% winners
2nd	28% winners
3rd	13% winners
4th	10% winners
Unplaced	24% winners
ALL SELECTIONS	23% winners

The 24% recorded by horses unplaced last time out is really not so surprising when you consider that there are many more of them than any other category, but clearly firsts and seconds on their previous outing did best. No category can be completely ignored, but with winning percentages of 39 and 28 respectively, winners and seconds last time out are obviously a cut above the rest and should be given special attention.

Finally, selections were analysed with regard to whether they ran in handicaps or non-handicaps. We have already seen that, in general, handicappers are always much less reliable propositions and this was underlined by the survey:

Non-handicaps	33%	winners
Handicaps	13%	winners
ALL SELECTIONS	23%	winners

To sum up, the overall 23% from all selections may seem disappointing, compared with say the 45%–50% to be had from favourites in certain kinds of races. However, it must be remembered that, unlike favourites, not all winning press selections start at short odds – they win at all prices up to 20-1, even if the majority are at the lower end of the scale. There will always be a level-stake loss on all selections over a reasonable period, but selectivity clearly pays. The survey revealed three main areas in which discrimination could be exercised:

1: Horses priced from 5-2 to 4-1 offer excellent value.
2: It is best to concentrate on winners and seconds last time out.
3: It pays to ignore handicaps.

As is the case with any way of betting on horses, press selections do not instantly promise quick riches. Of the three possible avenues of approach – naps, the consensus factor and selections race-by-race – almost certainly the best is to single out one correspondent and follow his selections on the basis of the selective criteria summarized above. You will never become a millionaire by adopting this method, but you do stand a sporting chance of coming out on the right side.

THE QUESTION OF STAKING

There is perhaps no more vexed question in betting circles than the desirability or otherwise of using staking plans. Certainly it is vital to regulate stakes on a rational basis, even if this goes no further than a rigid commitment to level stakes. If we consider the opposite course, namely that of staking varying amounts according to fancy, it soon becomes apparent that sensibly regulated staking must always be superior. I dare say that before you began reading this book you made selections based on your own reading of form and staked in what can only be described as a haphazard fashion, a large stake on what you considered an outstanding prospect, smaller amounts on horses which seemed to have less chance. In other words, in the matter of staking, you were governed solely by your own whim. What usually happened? I can imagine. You backed your share of winners, but probably lost in the long run. Why? Almost certainly because much of the time large stakes were dissipated on losers and when you backed a winner you had a lesser amount on. Of course this did not happen on every occasion, but if you look back on much of your betting, you will probably have to admit that more often than not it corresponded to this fatal pattern. In short, it is not the winners you back that matters in the long run, but how you back them. The secret of winning at racing must always be proper staking.

Sensibly regulated staking must always be superior. The keyword here is 'sensibly', for many staking plans are far from sensible. There can be no more effective lesson for the newcomer to stake-adjustment formulas than to examine at some length two of the most popular, and also the silliest, strategies for 'certain' profits from racing. I refer to 'doubling up' and 'retrieve' staking.

Both methods depend on increasing stakes after losers, the most common form of staking plan. The idea is to increase stakes on a losing run in the hope that the winner which terminates it will recoup all losses and produce a profit on the sequence as a whole. There are two points which are suspect about this. First, the losing run may be unduly prolonged and second, the price of the winner when it finally turns up may be too short to achieve this goal. In either case, or more precisely in a combination of both, the return accruing from the winner may be insufficient to regain what has been sacrificed on the losers.

The 'doubling up' idea well illustrates these points. Stakes are doubled after each loser until a winner occurs when, it is hoped, all previous losses will be wiped out and a profit shown. To understand the dangers attendant upon such a plan, examine the following sequence of bets:

STAKE	RESULT	WIN	LOSE	TOTAL PROFIT (+) or LOSS (−)
£1	Lost		£1	− £1
£2	Lost		£2	− £3
£4	Lost		£4	− £7
£8	Lost		£8	− £15
£16	Lost		£16	− £31
£32	Won 4-9	£14.22		− £16.78
£1	Lost		£1	− £17.78
£2	Lost		£2	− £19.78
£4	Lost		£4	− £23.78
£8	Lost		£8	− £31.78
£16	Lost		£16	− £47.78
£32	Lost		£32	− £79.78
£64	Lost		£64	− £143.78
£128	Lost		£128	− £271.78
£256	Lost		£256	− £527.78
£512	Lost		£512	− £1039.78
£1024	Won 2-1	£2048		+ £1008.22

This sequence of seventeen bets amply demonstrates the very grave risks involved in the system of 'doubling up'. After the first winner in the series, its price, that is 9-4 on, was not good enough to recoup the losses arising from only five losers. The next losing run was terminated by a winner which did regain all losses and produced a profit, but who can begin betting with £1 and only a short time later cheerfully stake £1,024? Moreover, if that bet had gone down, the next stake required would have been a little matter of £2,048! In short, no backer's capital, unless he possessed almost limitless means, could stand this kind of lunatic increasing of stakes.

It could be argued that a losing run of ten is impossible. If you believe that, then you have not been very long at the racing game. Of course if you confine yourself to short-priced selections with a high percentage of winners, such a sequence is unlikely, but, I emphasize, still not impossible. Moreover, even then the most probable outcome is what actually happened with the first winner in the example: odds too short to recover earlier losses.

Clearly, rapid increasing of stakes after losers is the road to financial ruin sooner or later. 'Doubling up' is the simplest way to commit betting suicide.

Exactly the same kind of risks accompany 'retrieve' or, as it is sometimes called, 'cover-to-win' staking. In such systems the backer aims to win a fixed sum should his selection prove successful. If it loses, the deficit from the first bet is added to the sum to be won and stakes adjusted accordingly on the next selection. Another loser means a further adjustment of stakes to regain all losses plus the sum initially fixed as the target figure, and so on. This is often billed as an 'infallible' system and so it is if, and it is a big if, the operator's capital is virtually without limit. Overleaf is an example of retrieve staking worked on an actual run of naps by a newspaper corresondent.

This may seem horribly complicated at first sight, but in fact is really quite simple. The target is to win £1 on every sequence of bets. After each loser in the series the lost stake is added to the accumulated deficit in the 'total profit or loss' column; the original £1 target is also

GOAL	PRICE	STAKE	RESULT	WIN	LOSE	TOTAL PROFIT (+) or LOSS(−)
£1	6-4	£0.67	Lost		£0.67	− £0.67
£1.67	2-1	£0.84	Lost		£0.84	− £1.51
£2.51	4-1	£0.63	Lost		£0.63	− £2.14
£3.14	4-5	£3.93	Lost		£3.93	− £6.07
£7.07	1-1	£7.07	Lost		£7.07	− £13.14
£14.14	5-2	£5.66	Lost		£5.66	− £18.80
£19.80	1-2	£39.60	Lost		£39.60	− £58.40
£59.40	13-8	£36.55	Lost		£36.55	− £94.95
£95.95	4-7	£167.91	Lost		£167.91	− £262.86
£263.86	8-11	£362.81	Won	£263.86		+ £1
				£263.86		

added to this amount and the total is then transferred to the 'goal' column to give the sum to be won on the next bet which will clear all losses so far and still produce a profit of £1 on the series as a whole.

The formula for calculating how much must be placed on a horse at any given price to produce the amount in the 'goal' column is not difficult. Simply reverse the two figures in the price of the horse and multiply. Thus on the first bet in the sequence the goal is £1. Reversing 6-4 we get $\frac{4}{6}$. Multiplying £1 by $\frac{4}{6}$ gives £0.67, which is the amount to be staked on the first horse.

At the end of the series the accumulated deficit in the 'total profit or loss' column has become £262.86. The target is still £1 profit on the sequence, so the amount to be transferred to the 'goal' column is £262.86 plus £1 equals £263.86. The price of the next horse is 8-11. Reversing the two figures gives $\frac{11}{8}$. £263.86 × $\frac{11}{8}$ equals £362.81. The horse wins, yielding the goal of £263.86, so the accumulated loss of £262.86 is written off and there is still a profit of £1 on the completed sequence.

Therefore on this series of ten bets you would have been required to risk £625.67 (£262.86 plus £362.81) to win £1. That is not my idea of a sound investment and I think little more needs to be said.

All staking plans which increase after losers run the risks to which I have drawn attention above. It is largely a matter of degree. For instance, a formula calling for a gradual increase of stakes against a losing run will usually improve the overall cash position in the backer's favour when compared with level stakes, but there will be times when the reverse will apply, namely when a losing run of lengthy duration sets in. For those who are prepared to take a calculated risk in their staking, however, here are some simple ideas which have more in their favour than against them:

Short-priced selections

Favourites etc. 45–50% winners. Maximum losing run expectancy: 5–6 bets.

Stake on the progression 112233, reverting to 1 after a winner or six consecutive losers, where 1 is 1 point, 2 is 2 points and 3 is 3 points.

Middle-priced selections

Horses priced 3-1 to 5-1. 25–30% winners. Maximum losing run expectancy: 9-10 bets.

Stake on the progression 1111122233, reverting to 1 after a winner or ten consecutive losers, where 1 is 1 point, 2 is 2 points and 3 is 3 points.

Long-priced selections

Horses priced around 10-1. 10% winners. Maximum losing run expectancy: 20–25 bets.

Stake on the progression 11111111112222 22333344455667, reverting to 1 after a winner or 28 consecutive losers, where 1 is 1 point, 2 is 2 points, 3 is 3 points, etc.

For readers who are unfamiliar with progressions which involve gradual increases in stakes after losers, below is a 20-bet series on short-priced horses. It is incidentally an extremely unfavourable sequence and by no means typical of the potential of a sound system based on favourites. However, it fully illustrates all the principles involved in the operation of this kind of formula.

	STAKE	RESULT	WIN	LOSE	TOTAL PROFIT (+) or LOSS (−)
1.	£1	Won 5-2	£2.50		+ £2.50
2.	£1	Lost		£1	+ £1.50
3.	£1	Lost		£1	+ £0.50
4.	£2	Won 7-4	£3.50		+ £4
5.	£1	Lost		£1	+ £3
6.	£1	Lost		£1	+ £2
7.	£2	Lost		£2	——
8.	£2	Lost		£2	− £2
9.	£3	Won 100-30	£10		+ £8
10.	£1	Lost		£1	+ £7
11.	£1	Won 6-4	£1.50		+ £8.50
12.	£1	Won 9-4	£2.25		+ £10.75
13.	£1	Lost		£1	+ £9.75
14.	£1	Lost		£1	+ £8.75
15.	£2	Lost		£2	+ £6.75
16.	£2	Lost		£2	+ £4.75
17.	£3	Lost		£3	+ £1.75
18.	£3	Lost		£3	− £1.25
19.	£1	Won 3-1	£3		+ £1.75
20.	£1	Won 15-8	£1.87		+ £3.62

The basic formula of increasing against a losing run on the progression 112233, reverting to 1 after a winner or six consecutive losers is, therefore, not difficult to apply. After bet 3 two consecutive losers calls for an increase to a 2-point stake on the fourth bet. This wins, so the stake immediately reverts to 1 point. The next losing run – bets 5 to 8 – sees the stake advance by degrees until a 3-point stake on bet 9 wins at 100-30 and causes the stake to go back to 1 point. Again on bets 13–18 there is another losing run, this time of six, which sees the 112233 progression stretched to the limit. Six consecutive losers are backed, but since stakes are never advanced beyond 3 points, the next bet on number 19 in the sequence reverts to 1 point. The series is brought to an end by a further 1 point on bet number 20 which happens to be a winner. If the sequence were continuing, the stake would be held at 1 point until the next run of two consecutive losers calls for an increase to 2 points.

The progressions for middle-priced and long-priced selections work in exactly the same way, except that the increases in stakes are more gradual and longer losing runs are allowed for, in accordance with what will probably happen in the light of the expected percentage of winners.

These three formulas are all versions of what the roulette player would call a 'losing martingale'. They will work very well most of the time. Much depends on the price of the winner which breaks the losing sequence, as well as on the length of the losing run, but provided that returns correspond to the expected norms for the type of selection being used, they are in the main effective. They are certainly a lot better than some more sophisticated schemes which depend for success on the occurrence of patterns of results which cannot be accurately predicted at the beginning of a sequence. As a calculated risk in increasing level-stake profits, they are worthy of cautious recommendation.

The opposite idea to that set out above is to increase stakes after winners. Here the fundamental idea is that you are betting with the bookmaker's money and not your own. Certainly the principle involves much less risk than increasing after losers, but there are a number of factors which make it less attractive than it appears at first sight. Because there is much less risk there is a corresponding reduction in profit potential – you may never acquire enough of the bookmaker's cash to make playing it up a worthwhile exercise.

Let us examine one of what I regard as one of the best of such formulas:

> Initial stake 5 points. Increase by 1 point after a winner and decrease by 2 points after a loser. Never drop the stake below 2 points.

This is designed to maximize profits from winners, while dropping stakes sharply once a sequence of losers occurs. Let us see what happens on a reasonably favourable sequence of results:

STAKE	RESULT	WIN	LOSE	TOTAL PROFIT (+) or LOSS (−)
£5	Won 2-1	£10		+ £10
£6	Lost		£6	+ £4
£4	Won 9-4	£9		+ £13
£5	Lost		£5	+ £8
£3	Lost		£3	+ £5
£2	Won 4-6	£1.33		+ £6.33
£3	Won 11-10	£3.30		+ £9.63
£4	Won 6-5	£4.80		+ £14.43
£5	Won 5-2	£12.50		+ £26.93
£6	Won 8-13	£3.69		+ £30.62
£7	Lost		£7	+ £23.62
£5	Won 6-4	£7.50		+ £31.12
£6	Lost		£6	+ £25.12

On the face of it, this is a very satisfactory result, but it is worth pointing out that a simple £5 level stake on the 13-bet sequence would have produced a profit of £34.16. Now let us rearrange the pattern of results in such a way that it is not so favourable to the staking plan:

STAKE	RESULT	WIN	LOSE	TOTAL PROFIT (+) or LOSS (−)
£5	Won 2-1	£10		+ £10
£6	Lost		£6	+ £4
£4	Won 9-4	£9		+ £13
£5	Lost		£5	+ £8
£3	Won 4-6	£2		+ £10
£4	Won 11-10	£4.40		+ £14.40
£5	Lost		£5	+ £9.40
£3	Won 6-5	£3.60		+ £13
£4	Lost		£4	+ £9
£2	Won 5-2	£5		+ £14
£3	Lost		£3	+ £11
£2	Won 8-13	£1.23		+ £12.23
£3	Won 6-4	£4.50		+ £16.73

Here the profit position worsens from £25.12 to £16.73, while the level-stake gain remains at £34.16. In short, plans which increase after winners only boost profits when the selection method produces long sequences of winners, and on this short sequence of thirteen bets, a run of five winners still did not produce a profit to match that accruing from level stakes. Moreover, most sequences are punctuated by fairly frequent losers.

This complete dependence on pattern makes any plan which increases after winners a suspect proposition. Take, for example, another staking formula of this type which, it has been claimed, completely eradicates the losing run:

> No bet until a winner occurs. Stake 1 point on the next bet and go on increasing by 1 point until a loser turns up. Then cease betting until the next winner and repeat the procedure.

But examine this sequence:

Won
Lost
Won
Lost
Won
Lost
Won
Lost
Won
Lost
Won
Lost
Won

Therefore, despite finding no less than seven winners in the 13-bet sequence, the operator of the above formula would have backed six consecutive losers.

Certainly plans calling for increases after winners reduce the risk to the backer, but worthwhile profits depend on strings of consecutive winners. These seldom occur in practice – winners and losers tend to alternate fairly regularly. Most of the time you are better off at level stakes.

I come now to what might be called 'reinvestment of profits', an approach which embodies much of my own personal philosophy of staking. The whole theme of this book has been to underline the need to bet along businesslike lines. Let us look at how a successful businessman proceeds. He might begin in a small way and after a reasonable period of time should have accumulated a fair amount of capital from the profits of his business. If he is to expand, he must plough back some of this capital. This he does, and as long as things continue to go well, profits go on increasing. Again, after a pause for consolidation, he expands further by putting back more accumulated profits into his enterprise. This is the way of successful business and I am firmly convinced that the man who backs horses should proceed along the same lines.

In betting terms this is of course basically a form of increasing stakes after winners. The difference, and it is a very big difference, is that the method of reinvesting profits I shall explain is quite unlike a rapidly fluctuating staking formula which, as I have tried to show above, seldom succeeds, because of its dependence on the occurrence of a particular kind of pattern, namely runs of winners falling together in sequence and unbroken by losers. In the 'reinvestment' formula set out below, it does not matter whether winners fall together in groups or are spread over the sequence punctuated by frequent losers. The reinvestment formula is altogether a more simple and, I believe, more effective concept than orthodox methods which increase stakes after winners.

Here is a formula for sequences involving single bets on favourites or near favourites:

1: Examine the state of profit or loss on a sequence every ten bets, that is after bet number 10, bet number 20, bet number 30 and so on.

2: If a worthwhile profit is being shown at each stage of review, increase stakes according to the following scale:

At least 6 points profit – stake an additional $\frac{1}{2}$ point on each selection over the next ten bets.

At least 12 points profit – stake an additional 1 point on each selection over the next ten bets.

At least 18 points profit – stake an additional $1\frac{1}{2}$ points on each selection over the next ten bets.

At least 24 points profit – stake an additional 2 points on each selection over the next ten bets.

Further increases should be made in proportion thus:

	30 points profit plus $2\frac{1}{2}$ points for 10 bets
	36 points profit plus 3 points for 10 bets
Showing	42 points profit plus $3\frac{1}{2}$ points for 10 bets
	48 points profit plus 4 points for 10 bets
	54 points profit plus $4\frac{1}{2}$ points for 10 bets
	60 points profit plus 5 points for 10 bets

These are level-stakes increases

This may be an entirely new concept to many readers, so here is a complete example worked out over a single-bet sequence on short-priced selections:

	STAKE	RESULT	WIN	LOSE	TOTAL PROFIT (+) or LOSS (−)
1.	£1	Won 3-1	£3		+ £3
2.	£1	Lost		£1	+ £2
3.	£1	Won 13-8	£1.62		+ £3.62
4.	£1	Won 7-2	£3.50		+ £7.12
5.	£1	Lost		£1	+ £6.12
6.	£1	Won 1-2	£0.50		+ £6.62
7.	£1	Lost		£1	+ £5.62
8.	£1	Won 6-4	£1.50		+ £7.12
9.	£1	Won 8-11	£0.73		+ £7.85
10.	£1	Lost		£1	+ £6.85

State of profit or loss after ten bets: more than 6 points profit but less than 12 points. Therefore, increase stakes by $\frac{1}{2}$ point over the next ten bets.

	STAKE	RESULT	WIN	LOSE	TOTAL PROFIT (+) or LOSS (−)
11.	£1+£0.50	Won 11-8	£2.06		+£8.91
12.	£1+£0.50	Lost		£1.50	+£7.41
13.	£1+£0.50	Lost		£1.50	+£5.91
14.	£1+£0.50	Lost		£1.50	+£4.41
15.	£1+£0.50	Won 9-4	£3.37		+£7.78
16.	£1+£0.50	Lost		£1.50	+£6.28
17.	£1+£0.50	Lost		£1.50	+£4.78
18.	£1+£0.50	Won 8-13	£0.92		+£5.70
19.	£1+£0.50	Lost		£1.50	+£4.20
20.	£1+£0.50	Won evens	£1.50		+£5.70

State of profit or loss after a further ten bets: less than 6 points. Therefore, reduce the stake to the original £1 over the next ten bets.

	STAKE	RESULT	WIN	LOSE	TOTAL PROFIT (+) or LOSS (−)
21.	£1	Won 7-4	£1.75		+£7.45
22.	£1	Lost		£1	+£6.45
23.	£1	Won 5-2	£2.50		+£8.95
24.	£1	Lost		£1	+£7.95
25.	£1	Lost		£1	+£6.95
26.	£1	Won 5-2	£2.50		+£9.45
27.	£1	Lost		£1	+£8.45
28.	£1	Won evens	£1		+£9.45
29.	£1	Won 15-8	£1.87		+£11.32
30.	£1	Won 8-11	£0.73		+£12.05

State of profit or loss after a further ten bets: more than 12 points profit but less than 18 points. Therefore, increase stakes by 1 point over the next ten bets.

	STAKE	RESULT	WIN	LOSE	TOTAL PROFIT (+) or LOSS (−)
31.	£1 + £1	Lost		£2	+ £10.05
32.	£1 + £1	Lost		£2	+ £8.05
33.	£1 + £1	Won 6-5	£2.40		+ £10.45
34.	£1 + £1	Lost		£2	+ £8.45
35.	£1 + £1	Won 2-1	£4		+ £12.45
36.	£1 + £1	Lost		£2	+ £10.45
37.	£1 + £1	Won 3-1	£6		+ £16.45
38.	£1 + £1	Lost		£2	+ £14.45
39.	£1 + £1	Won 5-4	£2.50		+ £16.95
40.	£1 + £1	Lost		£2	+ £14.95

State of profit or loss after a further ten bets: more than 12 points profit but less than 18 points. Therefore, hold the stake at an additional 1 point over the next ten bets.

	STAKE	RESULT	WIN	LOSE	TOTAL PROFIT (+) or LOSS (−)
41.	£1+£1	Won 2-1	£4		+£18.95
42.	£1+£1	Lost		£2	+£16.95
43.	£1+£1	Lost		£2	+£14.95
44.	£1+£1	Won 4-5	£1.60		+£16.55
45.	£1+£1	Lost		£2	+£14.55
46.	£1+£1	Won 11-4	£5.50		+£20.05
47.	£1+£1	Lost		£2	+£18.05
48.	£1+£1	Won 5-4	£2.50		+£20.55
49.	£1+£1	Lost		£2	+£18.55
50.	£1+£1	Won 5-2	£5		+£23.55

State of profit or loss after a further ten bets: more than 18 points but less than 24 points profit. Therefore, increase stakes by an additional 1½ points over the next ten bets.

	STAKE	RESULT	WIN	LOSE	TOTAL PROFIT (+) or LOSS (−)
51.	£1+£1.50	Lost		£2.50	+£21.05
52.	£1+£1.50	Won 100-30	£8.33		+£29.38
53.	£1+£1.50	Won 4-9	£1.11		+£30.49
54.	£1+£1.50	Lost		£2.50	+£27.99
55.	£1+£1.50	Won 6-4	£3.75		+£31.74
56.	£1+£1.50	Lost		£2.50	+£29.24
57.	£1+£1.50	Won 5-4	£3.12		+£32.36
58.	£1+£1.50	Lost		£2.50	+£29.86
59.	£1+£1.50	Won 5-2	£6.25		+£36.11
60.	£1+£1.50	Won 11-10	£2.75		+£38.86

Thus the reinvestment formula improves the level-stake profit position of £24.30 by just over 50%. This is a very satisfactory outcome. Clearly, ploughing back profits at predetermined points in a successful sequence pays dividends.

The reinvestment formula can be applied equally

well to middle-priced and long-priced selections. Because likely losing runs are greater than for favourites and near-favourites, however, there must be some modification in the scales of increase which need to be less volatile. My recommendations are:

Middle-priced selections

	9 points profit extra $\frac{1}{2}$ point for 12 bets
	18 points profit extra 1 point for 12 bets
	27 points profit extra $1\frac{1}{2}$ points for 12 bets
	36 points profit extra 2 points for 12 bets
Showing	45 points profit extra $2\frac{1}{2}$ points for 12 bets
	54 points profit extra 3 points for 12 bets
	63 points profit extra $3\frac{1}{2}$ points for 12 bets
	72 points profit extra 4 points for 12 bets
	81 points profit extra $4\frac{1}{2}$ points for 12 bets
	90 points profit extra 5 points for 12 bets

Long-priced selections

	12 points profit extra $\frac{1}{2}$ point for 15 bets
	24 points profit extra 1 point for 15 bets
	36 points profit extra $1\frac{1}{2}$ points for 15 bets
	48 points profit extra 2 points for 15 bets
Showing	60 points profit extra $2\frac{1}{2}$ points for 15 bets
	72 points profit extra 3 points for 15 bets
	84 points profit extra $3\frac{1}{2}$ points for 15 bets
	96 points profit extra 4 points for 15 bets
	108 points profit extra $4\frac{1}{2}$ points for 15 bets
	120 points profit extra 5 points for 15 bets

Here is an example on a test sequence of 36 bets, using middle-priced selections:

	STAKE	RESULT	WIN	LOSE	TOTAL PROFIT (+) or LOSS (−)
1.	£1	Lost		£1	− £1
2.	£1	Lost		£1	− £2
3.	£1	Won 5-1	£5		+ £3
4.	£1	Lost		£1	+ £2
5.	£1	Won 9-2	£4.50		+ £6.50
6.	£1	Lost		£1	+ £5.50
7.	£1	Won 5-2	£2.50		+ £8
8.	£1	Lost		£1	+ £7
9.	£1	Lost		£1	+ £6
10.	£1	Lost		£1	+ £5
11.	£1	Won 7-1	£7		+ £12
12.	£1	Lost		£1	+ £11

State of profit or loss after 12 bets: more than 9 points profit but less than 18 points. Therefore, increase stakes by $\frac{1}{2}$ point over the next 12 bets.

	STAKE	RESULT	WIN	LOSE	TOTAL PROFIT (+) or LOSS (−)
13.	£1+£0.50	Won 7-2	£5.25		+£16.25
14.	£1+£0.50	Lost		£1.50	+£14.75
15.	£1+£0.50	Lost		£1.50	+£13.25
16.	£1+£0.50	Lost		£1.50	+£11.75
17.	£1+£0.50	Lost		£1.50	+£10.25
18.	£1+£0.50	Won 4-1	£6		+£16.25
19.	£1+£0.50	Lost		£1.50	+£14.75
20.	£1+£0.50	Lost		£1.50	+£13.25
21.	£1+£0.50	Lost		£1.50	+£11.75
22.	£1+£0.50	Lost		£1.50	+£10.25
23.	£1+£0.50	Won 9-2	£6.75		+£17
24.	£1+£0.50	Lost		£1.50	+£15.50

State of profit or loss after a further 12 bets: more than 12 points profit but less than 18 points. Therefore, hold the stake at an additional $\frac{1}{2}$ point over the next 12 bets.

	STAKE	RESULT	WIN	LOSE	TOTAL PROFIT (+) or LOSS (−)
25.	£1+£0.50	Won 100-30 £5			+£20.50
26.	£1+£0.50	Lost		£1.50	+£19
27.	£1+£0.50	Lost		£1.50	+£17.50
28.	£1+£0.50	Lost		£1.50	+£16
29.	£1+£0.50	Won 11-2	£8.25		+£24.25
30.	£1+£0.50	Lost		£1.50	+£22.75
31.	£1+£0.50	Lost		£1.50	+£21.25
32.	£1+£0.50	Won 3-1	£4.50		+£25.75
33.	£1+£0.50	Lost		£1.50	+£24.25
34.	£1+£0.50	Won 9-4	£3.37		+£27.62
35.	£1+£0.50	Lost		£1.50	+£26.12
36.	£1+£0.50	Lost		£1.50	+£24.62

If the sequence were continuing, there would now be an additional 1 point on each selection for the next 12 bets, since the profit has now exceeded 18 points but not reached 27 points. again the reinvestment method produces a highly acceptable increase in profits when measured against the level-stake position. Of course it is not certain to do so. A prolonged sequence where the balance of results is heavily against the backer will not only build up a sizeable deficit but also dissipate any earlier profits. However, provided the method of selection is sound and things go reasonably well, the reinvestment method should boost profits, often quite substantially over a lengthy successful run, when compared with level stakes.

Moreover, the formula can be combined with earlier suggestions for profit-boosting based on increasing stakes after losers. Examine this sequence where the first amount in the 'stake' column represents the 112233 formula and the second, the additional level-stakes increases called for under the reinvestment method. The sequence is of course based on short-priced selections:

	STAKE	RESULT	WIN	LOSE	TOTAL PROFIT (+) or LOSS (−)
1.	£1	Won 8-13	£0.61		+ £0.61
2.	£1	Lost		£1	− £0.39
3.	£1	Lost		£1	− £1.39
4.	£2	Won 3-1	£6		+ £4.61
5.	£1	Lost		£1	+ £3.61
6.	£1	Won 4-6	£0.66		+ £4.27
7.	£1	Lost		£1	+ £3.27
8.	£1	Lost		£1	+ £2.27
9.	£2	Won 2-1	£4		+ £6.27
10.	£1	Won 8-11	£0.73		+ £7

State of profit or loss after ten bets: more than 6 points profit but less than 12 points. Therefore, increase stakes by an additional $\frac{1}{2}$ point for the next ten bets. The 112233 formula operates independently of this level-stake increase until the next stage of review, that is until the next sequence of ten bets has been completed.

	STAKE	RESULT	WIN	LOSE	TOTAL PROFIT (+) or LOSS (−)
11.	£1+£0.50	Lost		£1.50	+£5.50
12.	£1+£0.50	Lost		£1.50	+£4
13.	£2+£0.50	Won 6-4	£3.75		+£7.75
14.	£1+£0.50	Won 5-2	£3.75		+£11.50
15.	£1+£0.50	Won 6-4	£2.25		+£13.75
16.	£1+£0.50	Lost		£1.50	+£12.25
17.	£1+£0.50	Lost		£1.50	+£10.75
18.	£2+£0.50	Won 2-1	£5		+£15.75
19.	£1+£0.50	Lost		£1.50	+£14.25
20.	£1+£0.50	Won 1-2	£0.75		+£15

State of profit or loss after a further ten bets: more than 12 points profit but less than 18 points. Therefore, increase stakes by an additional 1 point for the next ten bets.

STAKE	RESULT	WIN	LOSE	TOTAL PROFIT (+) or LOSS (−)
21. £1+£1	Lost		£2	+£13
22. £1+£1	Lost		£2	+£11
23. £2+£1	Won 9-4	£6.75		+£17.75
24. £1+£1	Won evens	£2		+£19.75
25. £1+£1	Lost		£2	+£17.75
26. £1+£1	Lost		£2	+£15.75
27. £2+£1	Lost		£3	+£12.75
28. £2+£1	Won 3-1	£9		+£21.75
29. £1+£1	Won 5-2	£5		+£26.75
30. £1+£1	Won 4-6	£1.33		+£28.08

State of profit or loss after a further ten bets: more than 24 points profit but less than 30 points. Therefore, increase stakes by an additional 2 points for the next ten bets.

	STAKE	RESULT	WIN	LOSE	TOTAL PROFIT (+) or LOSS (−)
31.	£1+£2	Lost		£3	+£25.08
32.	£1+£2	Lost		£3	+£22.08
33.	£2+£2	Lost		£4	+£18.08
34.	£2+£2	Lost		£4	+£14.08
35.	£3+£2	Lost		£5	+£9.08
36.	£3+£2	Won 6-4	£7.50		+£16.58
37.	£1+£2	Won 3-1	£9		+£25.58
38.	£1+£2	Won 5-2	£7.50		+£33.08
39.	£1+£2	Lost		£3	+£30.08
40.	£1+£2	Lost		£3	+£27.08

State of profit or loss after a further ten bets: more than 24 points profit but less than 30 points. Therefore, hold the stake at an additional 2 points for the next ten bets.

	STAKE	RESULT	WIN	LOSE	TOTAL PROFIT (+) or LOSS (−)
41.	£2+£2	Won 7-4	£7		+£34.08
42.	£1+£2	Won 10-11	£2.73		+£36.81
43.	£1+£2	Lost		£3	+£33.81
44.	£1+£2	Won 8-13	£1.85		+£35.66
45.	£1+£2	Lost		£3	+£32.66
46.	£1+£2	Lost		£3	+£29.66
47.	£2+£2	Lost		£4	+£25.66
48.	£2+£2	Won evens	£4		+£29.66
49.	£1+£2	Lost		£3	+£26.66
50.	£1+£2	Lost		£3	+£23.66

State of profit or loss after a further ten bets: more than 18 points profit but less than 24 points. Therefore, decrease stake to an additional 1½ points for the next ten bets.

	STAKE	RESULT	WIN	LOSE	TOTAL PROFIT (+) or LOSS (−)
51.	£2+£1.50	Won 7-2	£12.25		+£35.91
52.	£1+£1.50	Won evens	£2.50		+£38.41
53.	£1+£1.50	Won 10-11	£2.27		+£40.68
54.	£1+£1.50	Won evens	£2.50		+£43.18
55.	£1+£1.50	Lost		£2.50	+£40.68
56.	£1+£1.50	Lost		£2.50	+£38.18
57.	£2+£1.50	Won 6-4	£5.25		+£43.43
58.	£1+£1.50	Won 2-1	£5		+£48.43
59.	£1+£1.50	Lost		£2.50	+£45.93
60.	£1+£1.50	Won 11-4	£6.87		+£52.80

If the sequence were continuing, the additional stake for the next ten bets would be 4 points, since the total profit is more than 48 points but less than 54 points.

Thus there is no reason why the two methods should not be combined, assessing the additional level-stakes increases for each subsequent run of ten bets on the basis of total profits accumulated from the formula. This calls for the operation of the 112233 progression against a losing run, reverting to 1 point after a winner or six consecutive losers plus any earlier gains from the level stakes increases called for under the reinvestment method. Provided you maintain one stake column for the 112233 formula and one for the additional bets indicated by the reinvestment method, assessment of stakes at each stage of review for subsequent sequences of ten bets is not difficult.

Clearly the combination of the two methods can be very profitable. The final profit of £52.80 compares extremely favourably with the £17.34 achieved by £1 level stakes throughout the sequence. The losing run did not extend beyond the normal expectancy for favourites of five, but with a final profit of over £50 the system would have been well able to withstand a much longer adverse run.

The technique of combining the 112233 formula for favourites with the reinvestment method is a very sophisticated one. Clearly it can enhance profits very considerably. However, it is also a very volatile form of staking. For this reason it is absolutely vital to maintain a high percentage of winners when combining the two approaches. As for middle-priced selections, therefore, you would need to be very sure of yourself to operate the two methods together on the same sequence of selections and, in the case of outsiders, the probable percentage of winners would be too low to recommend such a procedure. It would be better to opt either for increasing stakes after losers according to the suggested formula or to employ the reinvestment method. The two together would present grave risks to the backer, given the almost certain occurrence of long losing runs from the outsider type of selection.

Throughout this chapter on staking I have been at some pains to stress the dangers as well as the advantages inherent in the use of stake-adjustment formulas. This is because a long losing run on which all betting enterprises may founder is a threat whose occurrence must always be considered as a possibility, however remote. Yet nothing can eradicate the consequences of a disastrous run of losers, whether you use a staking plan or not. Given the extreme difficulty of winning at racing, let me state in conclusion my belief that the use of staking plans can increase profits to such an extent that no backer who hopes to win a worthwhile sum can really do without them. Provided that reliable selection methods are used, staking plans, for better or worse, may be the only way to win consistently and well at racing.

YOUR BETTING BOOK

DATE	RACE MEETING	HORSE	PRICE	WIN		LOSE	

DATE	RACE MEETING	HORSE	PRICE	WIN	LOSE

DATE	RACE MEETING	HORSE	PRICE	WIN		LOSE	

DATE	RACE MEETING	HORSE	PRICE	WIN	LOSE

DATE	RACE MEETING	HORSE	PRICE	WIN		LOSE	

DATE	RACE MEETING	HORSE	PRICE	WIN		LOSE	

DATE	RACE MEETING	HORSE	PRICE	WIN	LOSE

DATE	RACE MEETING	HORSE	PRICE	WIN		LOSE	

DATE	RACE MEETING	HORSE	PRICE	WIN		LOSE	

DATE	RACE MEETING	HORSE	PRICE	WIN	LOSE

DATE	RACE MEETING	HORSE	PRICE	WIN		LOSE	